Asperger Syndrome
• An Owner's Manual •

Asperger Syndrome
• An Owner's Manual •

What You, Your Parents and Your Teachers Need to Know

An Interactive Guide and Workbook

Ellen S. Heller Korin, M.Ed.

APC

AAPC Publishing
6448 Vista Dr.
Shawnee, KS 66218
www.aapcpublishing.net

©2006 AAPC Publishing
6448 Vista Dr.
Shawnee, KS 66218
www.aapcpublishing.net

Publisher's Cataloging-in-Publication

Korin, Ellen S. Heller.

    Asperger syndrome--an owner's manual : what you, your parents and your teachers need to know / Ellen S. Heller Korin. -- 1st ed. -- Shawnee Mission, Kan. : Autism Asperger Pub. Co., 2006.

    p. ; cm.
    ISBN-13: 978-1-931282-91-8
    ISBN-10: 1-931282-91-9
    LCCN: 2006922711
    "An interactive guide and workbook."
    Audience: students grade 5-8 and their parents and teachers.

    1. Asperger's syndrome in children. 2. Asperger's syndrome in children--Handbooks, manuals, etc. 3. Autistic children--Behavior modification. 4. Asperger's syndrome in children--Treatment. I. Title.

RJ506.A9 .K67 2006
618.92/858832--dc22   0605

Designed in Helvetica Neue and American Typewriter.

Printed in the United States of America.

DEDICATION

This book is dedicated to the many wonderful people with Asperger Syndrome with whom I have had the privilege of working. You are all my heroes and heroines; I am\ gratified by your triumphs.

Especially for Michelle, who started it all …
Aimee, who inspired me to create this, and
for all the friends and family who supported and encouraged me.

And most of all, in memory of my parents, Alexander and Ruth, and my brother David, who would have "kvelled."

And in celebration of my husband, Jonathan, who supports and loves me no matter what … and my daughter, Alexandra, who lights up my world.

ACKNOWLEDGMENTS

There are many people who have contributed in some way to the evolution of this book. I'd first like to thank Michelle Phelan Knight, who introduced me to AS and who started me on this path; the AS community in the Boston area, including the Asperger Association of New England, Dan and Barbara Rosenn, Denise Grenier, Robin Montville, and the many other people in the AS community who have enriched my life.

I thank Keith Myles and Kirsten McBride, and all the folks at the Autism Asperger Publishing Company, for walking me through this process gently.

And finally, I thank my friends and family for the love and support they always give me.

PREFACE

This interactive workbook is designed for young people roughly from 5th to 8th grade. It is intended to be used with the guidance and assistance of a helping adult, rather than to be given to the youngster to complete independently. The helping adult can be a parent, trusted teacher or a clinician (guidance counselor, psychologist, speech/language specialist, etc.), or some combination thereof. The more "interaction" that is involved in developing the child's Personal Profile and plan, the richer the outcome is likely to be.

The purpose of the workbook is ...

- To provide some basic information about Asperger Syndrome
- To enable the young person to understand a little bit about his way of functioning – what helps, what hurts
- To reassure the young person that the things she is struggling with can improve
- To provide a concrete way to communicate needs to parents, teachers and others
- And most of all, to empower by giving the young person a chance to identify his needs and to participate in developing interventions and future plans

An excellent time to introduce the workbook is when the diagnosis of Asperger Syndrome (AS) has first been made and is being presented to the youngster. This is a good time to give the young person access to information about AS and afford him an opportunity to express his feelings about having gotten this "mysterious" diagnosis.

Another opportune moment is later on – after a reevaluation when the results are being explained to the child. It is astonishing how often children receive very little information. Many young people have almost no awareness of the strengths and weaknesses revealed by testing and no clear understanding of what accounts for some of the difficulties they experience. Parents and professionals tend to withhold information to "protect" the child. Although well intentioned, this limits the child's ability to engage in a process of problem solving.

Another very appropriate time to introduce the workbook is when a problem has come up and the child's motivation to communicate her needs is high; "how about telling (teacher, friend, relative, neighbor) a little about what makes you (upset, angry, etc.) and what helps? This workbook is a way to do that." If as a parent you are uncomfortable doing this, get help from the professionals working with the youth. It is important that the adult helping the student with this workbook is comfortable, positive and accepting.

Getting an AS diagnosis is like finally getting a road map after being lost and confused. You now have some information that can potentially lead to effective interventions and treatment. People with AS have many strengths and can learn about or compensate for many of the challenges they face. The person working with the student on this workbook must recognize and point out strengths while helping to identify problem areas and solutions.

WHY DO I NEED A WORKBOOK?

Well, let's think about it ...

- If you have been told you have Asperger Syndrome, often referred to as AS, you might have questions about how if affects you.

- You might want to understand AS and yourself better.

- You might want to know how to make difficult tasks easier for you.

- You might want to use your strengths more effectively.

- You might want to reach some goals that have been hard for you to achieve (like making friends).

- You may want to let the people in your world know more about the things that really matter to you, your learning and living profile and so on.

These are some of the things you can learn about and get answers to
by working through this workbook.

Can you think of other reasons (write them down below)?

_____

_____

_____

_____

What is your most important reason?

_____

_____

_____

_____

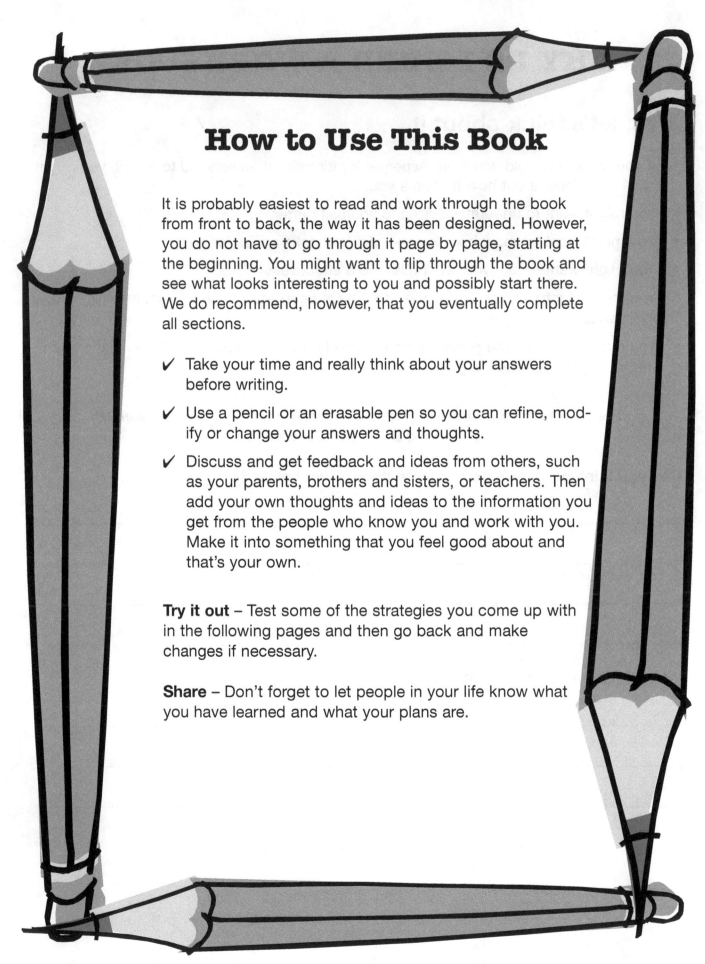

How to Use This Book

It is probably easiest to read and work through the book from front to back, the way it has been designed. However, you do not have to go through it page by page, starting at the beginning. You might want to flip through the book and see what looks interesting to you and possibly start there. We do recommend, however, that you eventually complete all sections.

✔ Take your time and really think about your answers before writing.

✔ Use a pencil or an erasable pen so you can refine, modify or change your answers and thoughts.

✔ Discuss and get feedback and ideas from others, such as your parents, brothers and sisters, or teachers. Then add your own thoughts and ideas to the information you get from the people who know you and work with you. Make it into something that you feel good about and that's your own.

Try it out – Test some of the strategies you come up with in the following pages and then go back and make changes if necessary.

Share – Don't forget to let people in your life know what you have learned and what your plans are.

WORDS YOU WILL NEED TO KNOW

CHARACTERISTICS (TRAITS) – a distinguishing feature of your personality (you may be shy, studious, etc.).

DISTRACTORS – things and activities that take your mind off of things – that tend to capture your attention.

DYSLEXIA – basic difficulty associating sounds with letters, which makes it very difficult to learn to read and spell. For example, people with dyslexia often see letters in reverse, making it difficult to read accurately; they may see the letter "b" as a "d" or reverse the order of letters in a word (frist for first).

LEARNING DISABILITY – a learning disability is something that interferes with learning in the typical way. There are many kinds of learning disabilities such as dyslexia (see above) or dyscalculia (interferes with math skills). People with learning disabilities have at least average learning ability and can learn to overcome or compensate for the interferences.

NONVERBAL – relating to visual (what you can see) or motor (hands-on) activities, as opposed to verbal – having to do with language.

SENSORY INPUT – the sounds, sights, smells that are in your immediate environment (that surround you).

SENSORY OVERLOAD – the feeling of being overwhelmed when there is too much going on around you (think of the hallways at change of classes or the school cafeteria at lunch time).

SOOTHERS – things and activities that calm you, such as listening to music or breathing deeply.

VERBAL – relating to the understanding and use of language. For example, being verbal means being good at using words, having a good vocabulary. Verbal skills are the skills related to language, like sounding out words, being able to express ideas in words (spoken or written), etc.

SOME BASICS

What Is Asperger Syndrome?

Everyone has a set of strengths and weaknesses. Some are good at reading, but not so great in math. Others excel at sports but struggle in school. *Everyone has a profile of strengths and weaknesses.*

Many people never get to know their profile because things tend to go relatively smoothly for them, and they never have the occasion to get tested. However, other folks (or their parents or teachers) notice that some things are more difficult for them than they expected. They want to know more about their skills and learning style. They might get tested to find out more specific information. They might also consult with specialists in learning and/or behavior.

When the result of such testing or consultation is a diagnosis of Asperger Syndrome, it means that the person has a particular profile of strengths and weaknesses. For example, he tends to be stronger in language skills than in visual or motor skills. He is smart but may seem to avoid or dislike socializing.

As you read about AS, remember that not everyone with AS has all the "symptoms" or behaviors. Just think about what you've noticed about yourself or what people have pointed out to you.

Keep an open mind – it's like the old sayings:
"It's what you don't know that will hurt you."

OR

"Not everything that is faced can be changed,
but nothing can be changed until it's faced."

There are many definitions of Asperger Syndrome. To make it even more confusing, there are as many differences in the behavior of people with AS as there are people with AS!

Let's see what the "experts" say:
- Asperger's syndrome (AS) is a pervasive developmental disorder commonly referred to as a form of "high-functioning" autism. Individuals with Asperger Syndrome are considered to have a higher intellectual capacity while suffering from a lower social capacity. "Asperger's syndrome" was named after Hans Asperger, an Austrian psychiatrist and pediatrician whose work was not internationally recognized until the 1990s.

Here's how some folks with AS describe it:

A young adult diagnosed with Asperger Syndrome tells people that she has a type of "social dyslexia." This, she feels, best describes what AS is like for her.

Many people with AS talk about feeling like "aliens" from another planet, not able to figure out what's going on in social situations and not understanding what's expected of them, what they should say or how they should act.

What do you think about what you've read so far?

_____

_____

_____

_____

More about AS ...

Some people with AS seem to be "book smart," but don't seem to have "common sense." They are often uncomfortable and awkward with people, especially people their own age. They might be very intelligent, yet not notice or be able to do some very simple things. For example, they might walk on the left side of the hallway at school when everyone else goes down the right-hand side and, therefore, bump into everyone. On the other hand, some people with AS might notice details, but not "get the big picture."

Some people with AS like to do things in a very particular way or in a certain order. They might get upset if someone tries to interrupt or change the way they do things, or when things don't go as planned.

Some people with AS talk about the same subject(s) all the time. Sometimes they seem to be "making a speech" rather than "having a conversation."

People with AS might have a hard time making friends. Sometimes they are teased by other kids.

Sports are sometimes difficult for people with AS, especially team sports.

Common Characteristics

Although no two people with Asperger Syndrome are exactly the same, there are some things they seem to have in common. Here are some of them.

- They need more breaks than other people.
- They need to know what's going to happen – sudden change can be upsetting.
- They find interactions with others hard work because they don't always know what to say or do.
- They get stressed easily.
- They need time to be alone – to rest and repair.
- They can't always keep up with the pace of those around them.
- They get overwhelmed when there is too much sensory input.
- They have very particular interests and may know a great deal about them.
- They need extra time for many things.
- They may have problems with:
  - writing
  - reading books they have not chosen
  - showing the work in math problems and
  - organizing their work
- They may have trouble making friends or getting along with others.

Where Do These Characteristics Come From?

YOUR BRAIN – Part 1
Everyone's got a brain, and each brain works in its own unique way. Doctors have noticed that the brains of people with AS work a little differently than the brains of people without AS. This is not necessarily a good or a bad thing. *It is just a difference that needs to be understood and addressed.*

YOUR BRAIN – Part 2
You know all those tests you have taken? Well, one of the things they show is that if you have AS you probably have stronger **verbal** skills than **nonverbal** skills.

This means that you do better when you can read or talk about things than when you have to "look and see" or "see and do" certain activities. For example, sometimes you don't see what's going on or understand what you see (in maps, charts, pictures or in life). You might have trouble drawing pictures, or making maps and charts. You might not be so good at catching a ball. On the other hand, you are probably an awesome reader.

You can help yourself understand the nonverbal world around you by:
- talking things through
- using words to describe or explain things you see
  TRY THIS: When you are on the playground or at the park, use words to describe

what is going on. Who is playing with who? What activities are going on? How are people acting toward each other? Where do you see someone who might want someone to come over to them? What group looks like it has enough people and might not welcome someone else. Using words to describe what you see may help you understand what is going on and what might be the best thing for you to do.

Or use words to describe what you see in a picture – try it with a picture of the water cycle in a science book. A trick to help you get the most information is to "be a camera" and zoom out for the big picture or main idea, and to zoom in for the details.

How are you feeling right now?

_____

_____

_____

Do you see yourself in some of the descriptions about AS?

_____

_____

_____

Which ones?

_____

_____

_____

_____

Do you feel like talking to someone about how you're feeling?

_____

Who?

_____

It's a lot to take in at once. You might need to take a break.

The Diagnosis is a Road Map

So you've been told you have Asperger Syndrome ...

What Does It Mean?

First of all, it means:

- **You're Smart** (it's part of the definition).
  Did you know that you have to have average to above-average ability to qualify for a diagnosis of Asperger Syndrome? In fact, many people with AS have SUPERIOR ability.

- **Some things are hard for you.** You probably knew you were smart but didn't understand why some tasks were so difficult for you. For example, now you can begin to understand why social interactions are such hard work and why so many things are stressful or upsetting to you.

- **It's the way your brain works.** The more you know about your own special style, the more you can figure out how to help yourself. It's not because you need to be "fixed." It's because you want to accomplish some goals or make your life less stressful.

  This workbook will help you understand yourself – what's easy and what's hard, how you do things and how you learn best. It will help you define your Personal Profile.

  Understanding your Personal Profile is the first step in the plan to achieve your goals. For example, if you know that it takes you a little time to think of an answer to a question – in class or in a conversation – you can make a plan to say something like, "give me a minute to think about that" to gain a little time. Pretty soon it will become very natural to ask for time to think.

Knowing how you do things or what works best for you will help you make good plans.

PART 1: GETTING TO KNOW YOURSELF

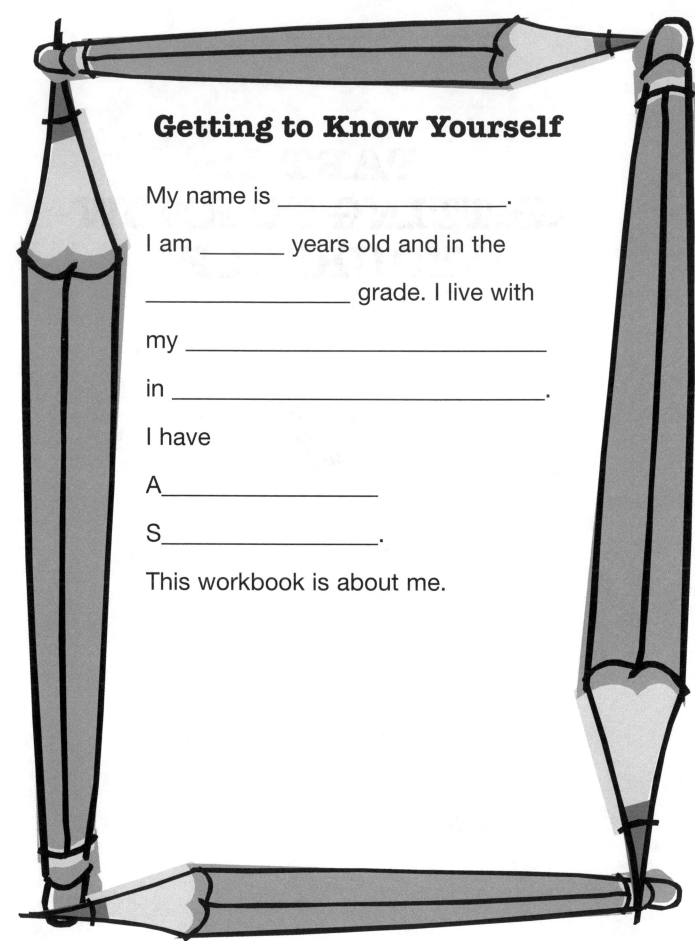

Getting to Know Yourself

My name is _____.

I am _____ years old and in the

_____ grade. I live with

my _____

in _____.

I have

A_____

S_____.

This workbook is about me.

THE REAL ME

Think about yourself.

- What is your way of doing things. Do you work slowly and carefully or do you rush through to get done?

- What do you like to do?

- What bothers you?

You will have the chance to tell about yourself on the pages coming up. You can ask someone who knows you well to help you. If someone helped you, write their name here:

_____ helped me to write about myself.

YOUR PERSONAL PROFILE – KNOW IT

Knowledge is power. If you know you are comforted by reading, for example, have a book handy all the time, especially when you expect things could get stressful. Or if you know that you get tired at holiday celebrations with all the noise and conversation, plan little breaks and "escapes" with your parents.

Knowing what you like and need is the beginning step in developing your Personal Plan to manage your AS.

So, Let's Get Started

You Find Some Things Easy and Do Them Well

List your strengths. *(For example: I am good at spelling. I am kind.)*

1. _____

   _____

   _____

2. _____

   _____

   _____

3. _____

   _____

   _____

4. _____

   _____

   _____

5. _____

   _____

   _____

You Find Other Things More Difficult

List some things that are hard for you. (*For example: It's hard for me to make friends. I have trouble with math.*)

1. _____

_____

_____

2. _____

_____

_____

3. _____

_____

_____

4. _____

_____

_____

5. _____

_____

_____

_____

Some Things Really Bother You

List the things that bother you. (*For example: I get upset when there is too much noise. I don't like people to get too close to me.*)

1. _____

_____

_____

2. _____

_____

_____

3. _____

_____

_____

4. _____

_____

_____

5. _____

_____

_____

On page 8, list things you dislike more intensely.

There Are Things You REALLY Don't Like

(These are things that you dislike more intensely; they more than bother or disturb you.)

List the things or activities you REALLY don't like. (*For example: I hate team sports. I really don't like to be told what to read.*)

1. _____

   _____

   _____

2. _____

   _____

   _____

3. _____

   _____

   _____

4. _____

   _____

   _____

5. _____

   _____

   _____

There Are Certain Things You REALLY, REALLY Like

List the things you love. (*For example: My favorite thing to do is fencing. I love to read science fiction or fantasy. I love "anime"!*)

1. _____

   _____

   _____

2. _____

   _____

   _____

3. _____

   _____

   _____

4. _____

   _____

   _____

5. _____

   _____

   _____

Some Things Really Comfort You

List the things that comfort/soothe you. (*For example: I love to read – it makes me feel calmer. I relax when I take a warm bath.*)

1. _____

_____

_____

2. _____

_____

_____

3. _____

_____

_____

4. _____

_____

_____

5. _____

_____

_____

Summary of Your Personal Profile

Fill in the spaces below using the information you wrote down on the previous pages.

My Strengths:

_____

_____

_____

_____

Things I Love:

_____

_____

_____

_____

Things That Calm Me:

_____

_____

_____

_____

LEARNING STYLE

Now let's look at the way you learn best. Everyone has a unique learning style. Let's take a look at yours.

• Ask the adult who is helping you with this workbook to tell you some of the things that people have noticed or that testing has shown about how you learn best.

List some of these things here:

_____

_____

_____

_____

Have you noticed some of the same things? Which ones?

_____

_____

_____

_____

Now it's your turn to figure out aspects of your learning style.

Are You a Good Detective?
What Can You Detect About Your Learning Style?

I understand and remember things better if I:

(Check the answer that fits you best)

☐ Read the information
☐ Listen to the information
☐ Do both
☐ Other: _____

_____

_____

_____

_____

I prefer to work:

(Check the answer that is true for you)

☐ In a group
☐ With the teacher or tutor
☐ By myself
☐ Other:

_____

_____

_____

_____

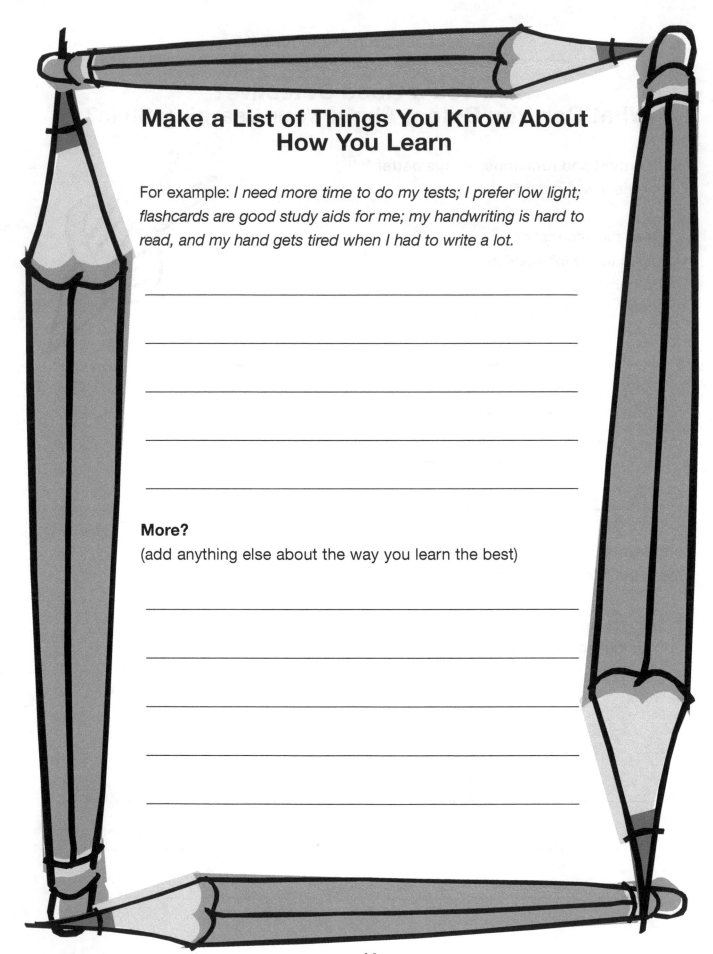

Make a List of Things You Know About How You Learn

For example: *I need more time to do my tests; I prefer low light; flashcards are good study aids for me; my handwriting is hard to read, and my hand gets tired when I had to write a lot.*

_____

_____

_____

_____

_____

More?

(add anything else about the way you learn the best)

_____

_____

_____

_____

_____

YOUR EMOTIONS

Emotions are the feelings that influence you. Sometimes you can control your emotions (for example, being able to stay in your seat at a Red Sox game even though you are excited about the win). Sometimes emotions seem to control you (you can't stop crying because you're very sad about something).

Emotions contribute to how and why we do things (for example, at the school dance you wonder if you have picked the right clothes or combed your hair enough. This makes you feel self-conscious, so you try not to be noticed and kind of hang back in the shadows).

Many times we worry about things even before they happen. Just thinking about having to go some place, or see someone, or do something can make us feel ANXIOUS. People with AS frequently experience a good deal of ANXIETY (feeling nervous and upset). Sometimes you know what you are anxious about (going to the dentist?), and sometimes it's just a general feeling of worry.

What makes you anxious? (taking tests, going shopping?)

_____

_____

_____

_____

_____

_____

_____

Tuning in to our emotions can help us survive in uncomfortable places and situations.

Here's an example: You need dressy clothes for a family wedding. You get overwhelmed in noisy, crowded department stores with so many choices. Knowing how you feel about big stores, you can plan to:
- Order from a catalog
- Go to a small specialty store where people help you to pick out and match clothes
- Have someone pre-select some outfits and either bring them home or have them held in the dressing room at the store so you can pick without having to go all over the store
- Go at off times when few people will be shopping

Again, knowing what you like or FEEL will help you make plans and arrangements that will work best for you.

There's another very important reason for getting to know your feelings:

Sometimes people with AS have trouble understanding feelings (like "love" and "caring") that other people talk about feeling toward their parents, friends and relatives. These words seem to lack meaning. But many people with AS want to understand and experience deep and meaningful connections and relationships with the people in their world. They just need some help to understand the idea and recognize the feelings. Learning about feelings and emotions can help you to make relationships more personal and help you to feel closer to the people you want to feel close to.

Your Emotions (Feelings):
How to Recognize Them – How to Understand Them

- **Do you know what it feels like to be ...**
  - ☐ Happy?
  - ☐ Calm?
  - ☐ Frustrated?
  - ☐ Sad?
  - ☐ Angry?
  - ☐ Nervous/anxious?

- **Can you tell what you are feeling at a particular moment in time?**

  _____

  _____

  _____

- **Can you tell what other people are feeling?**

  _____

  _____

  _____

It is important to learn how to do this.

Think about the following:
- When things are going smoothly, people usually feel CONTENT – or calm.
- When good things happen, people often feel HAPPY.
- What do you think people feel when things are going wrong – when they make mistakes? _____

Try to decide what you might feel when:
- Someone calls you a bad name or makes fun of you. _____
- You get a really good grade in school. _____
- Someone picks you to be on their team. _____
- You did your homework but left it at home. _____
- You can't find a seat in the lunchroom. _____
- You're going on vacation tomorrow. _____

Try to explain what the following words mean and what it feels like to be:

Happy (*For example, "happy means feeling good about what is going on; when I feel happy I am not worrying, I feel kind of calm but excited too."*): _____

_____

_____

Sad: _____

_____

_____

Angry: _____

_____

_____

Frustrated: _____

_____

_____

Annoyed: _____

_____

_____

Delighted: _____

_____

_____

Name some times when you felt each of these feelings (*for example, I was annoyed when my sister knocked my Legos down*): _____

_____

_____

Feelings and Relationships

Relationships can be complicated and confusing. Sometimes it's hard to tell how you feel about the people in your life. It's also hard to tell what other people are feeling about you. Being able to recognize and understand your feelings and other people's feelings can help you get along better with others and have the kind of relationships you would like to have with them.

Here are some good examples:

- You know you love your parents but you often get angry with them when they won't let you do what you want to do. It's confusing. Can you love and be angry with people at the same time? Absolutely! You can expect to feel all kinds of things in a real relationship.

- Sometimes you feel like being close, and sometimes you want to be alone. Sometimes you are annoyed or bothered by the people around you. You might admire someone and also feel jealous. Feelings are not "pure." You can have "mixed" emotions, or a combination of emotions. You can feel positive and negative emotions at the same time. *This is especially true in relationships with family members. These are usually the most important relationships, and they are the most complex.*

Use the rest of this page to make a list of feeling words that you can use to tell people how you are feeling.

_____

_____

_____

_____

_____

_____

_____

SENSORY ISSUES

Many people with Asperger Syndrome have difficulty with their five senses. They may find loud noises very upsetting. They may find clothes too tight or uncomfortable (some folks I know wear shorts and tee shirts in winter – even in the snow!). Some really don't like to be touched, especially not lightly; it startles them and makes them feel uncomfortable.

Do you notice any of these issues with:

Touching?

WHAT: _____

_____

_____

Tasting?

WHAT: _____

_____

_____

Hearing?

WHAT: _____

_____

_____

Seeing?

WHAT: _____

_____

_____

Smelling?

WHAT: _____

_____

_____

PART 2
USING THE
INFORMATION FROM
YOUR PERSONAL
PROFILE

Using the Information From Your Personal Profile

Now that you have gathered some information about yourself, you can start to think about ways to use it to help you do better at home, at school and with friends.

First you need goals.

What do you want to change about the way things are going for you?
For example, "I would like to be more organized" or I would like to have a friend."

_____

_____

_____

_____

What do you want people to know about you?
For example, "I'd like people to know that I sometimes don't know what to say and need a minute to think. I'm not ignoring them or being snobby; I really would like to talk with them."

_____

_____

_____

_____

What help do you need?
For example, "I need help with setting up my math problems so I don't make so many mistakes; or I need help to organize my binder and backpack because I can never find anything!"

_____

_____

_____

_____

What do you want to do on your own?

For example, "I would like to go to some classes in school without the teacher's aide." Or "I would like to try to ask the teacher for help myself rather than having my parents talk to her."

_____

_____

_____

_____

Many people with AS want to have friends, do better in school and get along better with family members.

What are your goals?

(write down some goals here)

_____

_____

_____

_____

_____

_____

_____

Putting It All Together

Review what you've just been thinking about and learned.

Explain what Asperger Syndrome means to you.

_____

_____

_____

_____

_____

Tell how you feel about having AS.

_____

_____

_____

_____

List some AS traits you've noticed in yourself.

_____

_____

_____

_____

_____

CREATE A PLAN USING YOUR PERSONAL PROFILE

Now you can make a personalized plan for achieving your goals. The plan is personalized because it includes some of the special things about you that you have listed in this workbook. For example, you love to read, so in your plan for school you ask for time to read to alleviate some of the stress and to take a break, when necessary.

Make your personalized plan for:
- A Good Learning Environment
- A Good Homework Environment
- Getting Along at Home
- Having Fun with Friends
- Preventing or Managing Meltdowns
  - An emergency kit
  - A plan at school
  - A plan at home
  - A way to keep your cool
  - A way to communicate your needs

My Personal Plan for the Best Learning Environment

Describe things you know help you to learn best.

Use the information you gathered about your learning style, preferences, likes and dislikes earlier.

I am most comfortable working (where) . . .

_____
_____
_____
_____
_____

I can focus best when . . .

_____
_____
_____
_____
_____
_____

If I get distracted, . . .

_____
_____
_____
_____
_____

I need help to . . .

_____
_____
_____
_____
_____
_____

My Personal Plan for the Best Homework Environment

Think about what you need in order to get your homework done with the least amount of stress.

Where have you been working?
Are there distractions? Is there a good workspace? Do you have all the materials and supplies you need? Is someone available to help if you need it?

Where do you think it is best for you to work? Maybe not your room, where you can easily "zone out" or become distracted. You might want to try different places before you decide, but once you have chosen a spot, set it up as a good workspace and use it all the time. You're less likely to lose track of things if you work in one place.

My best homework spot is:

_____

_____

When do you start your homework?
- Is it the same time each day, or does it depend on your extracurricular activities schedule?

_____

_____

- How do you decide what to do first? How much time do you spend on each assignment?

_____

_____

- Do you take breaks?

_____

_____

- Is there music playing or is the TV on?

_____

_____

- What do you do when you are finished with your homework?

_____

_____

The best time for me to do homework is:

_____

_____

For more ideas, see Successful Strategies, pages 52-54.

My Personal Homework Plan

With all the information you have just read, think of what works well for you and develop your personal homework plan.

MY PERSONAL HOMEWORK SCHEDULE

TIME	MONDAY	TUESDAY	WEDNESDAY	THURSDAY	FRIDAY
3:00					
4:00					
5:00					
6:00					
7:00					

I plan to work _____

I am going to use the Wonder Wheel system (see page 54) _____

I can ask _____ **for help.**

I can call _____

or go to this website _____ **for help.**

Other plans (snacks, rewards for finishing, etc.)

_____

_____

_____

28

My Personal Plan for Getting Along at Home

Think about what makes things go smoothly at home.
Write down some of the things that you notice help everyone get along.
For example, when everyone really listens to what someone else is saying before talking (or interrupting), it seems easier for the family to make decisions or to come to an agreement.

_____

_____

_____

Think of things that create problems at home.
Write down what creates problems:
• For your family members:

_____

_____

_____

• For you:

_____

_____

_____

Get Others' Points of View
Talk to your parent(s) and sibling(s) and ask what they think helps or hurts.
Collaborate. Put your thoughts and ideas together to make (and try out) a plan everyone thinks will help things go smoothly. Write down what you've learned:

_____

_____

_____

_____

_____

_____

What to Do

Write down what you think you and your family members can do to keep things going smoothly. Discuss these ideas with them to make your plan. Now write your family plan.

This is what we agree to do:

_____

_____

_____

_____

_____

_____

Have everyone sign this page to show that they agree. You might want to make a copy of your signed plan and post it on the fridge.

Signatures:

_____

_____

_____

_____

My Personal Plan for Having Fun With Friends

You probably have talked about how to get along with friends with your parents and other family members. You may have participated in groups designed to help you learn good social skills. You may know some of the "rules" for getting along well with others. For example, you probably know that it helps to look people in the eye, to smile and say hello, to take turns, to listen to what the other person says before answering or interrupting, etc. However, you may find it hard to do some of these things.

Can you do some of these? _____

Which ones? _____

_____

Which ones are difficult for you? _____

_____

Who can help you learn how to do these? _____

_____

Have you ever noticed anything else that seems to work well with friends? (It can be something you notice other people doing or something you have tried yourself.)

_____

_____

What do you do that you think may interfere with having fun with friends? Over the years your parents and teachers have probably told you what "not to do" with friends (for example, talking about only what you are interested in, acting superior, etc.). This might be hard to do, but try to describe some of the things you think you may do that interfere with good relationships with friends. You might want to get some help from adults with this. Don't be afraid to figure out what you are doing.

_____

_____

_____

Once you realize what might be getting in the way, you can figure out a way to change things to help you have the friends you want.

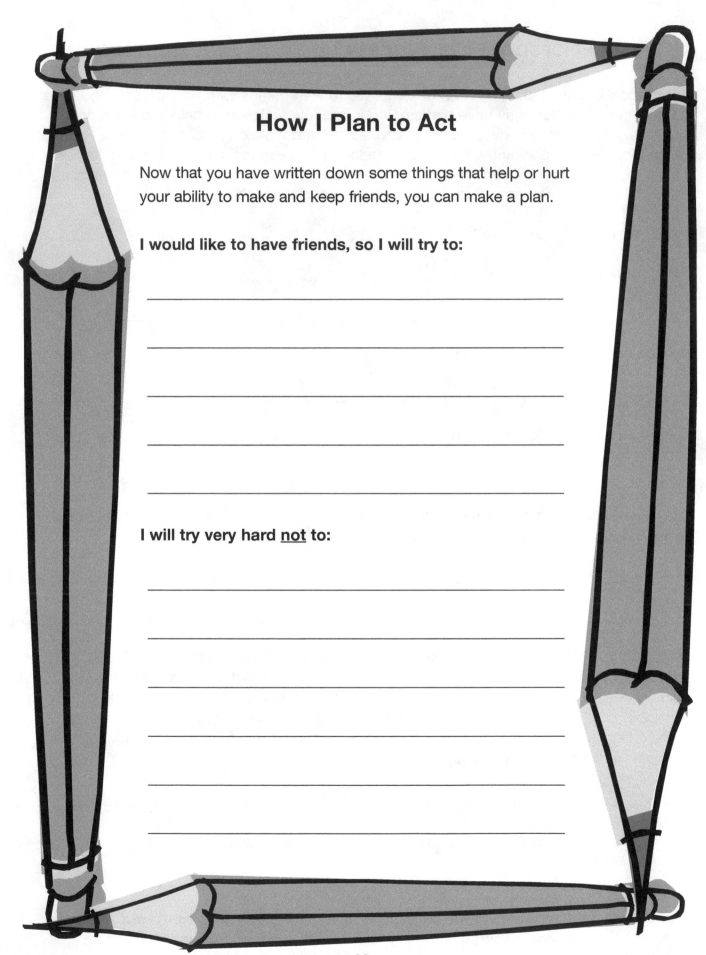

How I Plan to Act

Now that you have written down some things that help or hurt your ability to make and keep friends, you can make a plan.

I would like to have friends, so I will try to:

_____

_____

_____

_____

_____

I will try very hard <u>not</u> to:

_____

_____

_____

_____

_____

My Personal Plan to Prevent or Manage Meltdowns

In the middle of all our plans, "Life Happens." That is, no matter how well we plan, sometimes things happen to upset them. Things change, something unexpected comes up, things don't work out the way we thought they would, and so on. Maybe you planned to visit your grandparents over the holidays, but a snowstorm prevented you from going. Maybe you thought you did really well on your math test, but your score was lower than you expected.

People with AS tend to get upset more easily and/or more intensely than others. As a result, they need to have a plan to try to prevent, or at least minimize, meltdowns (extreme agitation, upset, anger).

To do this, it makes sense to:

- Make an emergency kit for those stressful times when you anticipate or realize you are overloaded or overwhelmed. *For more ideas, see Successful Strategies, pages 55-57.*

- Make a meltdown prevention plan for school and at home.

- Use the Meltdown Monitor to help you recognize and prevent meltdowns (see page 56).

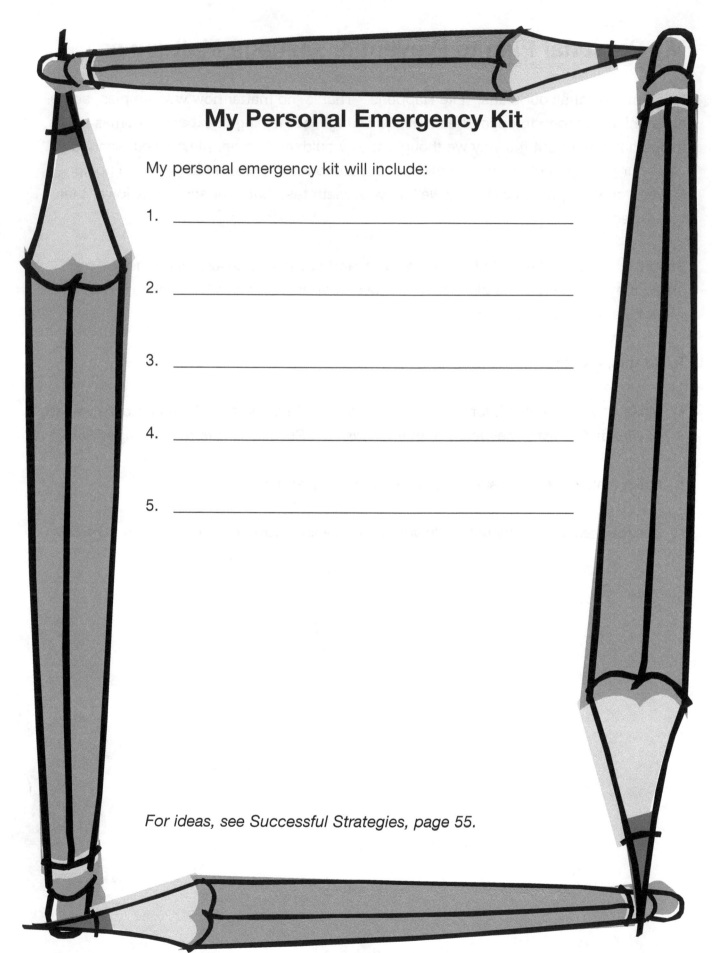

My Personal Emergency Kit

My personal emergency kit will include:

1. _____

2. _____

3. _____

4. _____

5. _____

For ideas, see Successful Strategies, page 55.

My Personal Home Meltdown Prevention Plan

Can you tell when you are getting really upset?

Many people can. If you can learn to do this, you might be able to avoid a total meltdown, or at least make meltdowns shorter and less intense.

Think about what you were feeling before you had your last big upset.

- Did you feel hot or cold?
- Did you begin to shake, or cough, or get a headache?

Write down your feelings here:

_____

_____

_____

_____

Try to notice all the feelings you have just before you "meltdown."
Write down your feelings here:

_____

_____

_____

_____

For help, turn to Successful Strategies, page 56.

When you feel a meltdown is on its way or has already begun, you can try some things that may help.

- GET AWAY from people.
- Do not – I repeat – do not try to resolve the conflict.
- Implement your plan!!

My Personal Plan at Home

I am learning how to tell when I am getting upset. I have discussed this with my parents and we have developed this plan.

If I am going to explode at home or if I start melting down,

I will go to_____

I will do _____

Also, I will_____

My parents and I agree that this is a good plan. They will remind me of the plan if I forget. Then they will let me have time to myself so I can calm myself down. They will not discuss the issue with me until I have calmed down.

I will not try to talk to them until I am calm.

My Personal School Meltdown Prevention Plan

School can be a very stressful place for people with AS. First of all, there's a busy, often hectic pace. Second, there are always lots of people around. It's especially crowded in the hallways and the lunchroom. Everyone is supposed to do the same things at the same time and at the same pace.

All these things together, or by themselves, can make you anxious, nervous or upset, which can lead to a meltdown.

What are some situations that you find especially stressful at school?

1. _____

_____

_____

2. _____

_____

_____

3. _____

_____

_____

4. _____

_____

_____

5. _____

_____

_____

For ideas on how to help prevent, or least diminish, meltdowns, see Successful Strategies, page 58.

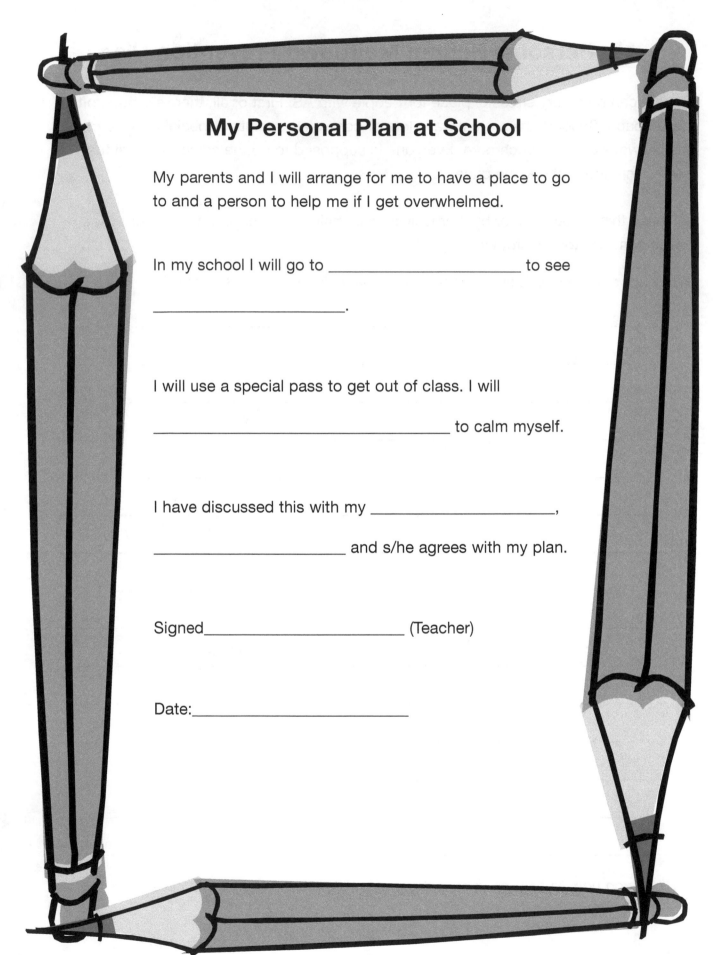

My Personal Plan at School

My parents and I will arrange for me to have a place to go to and a person to help me if I get overwhelmed.

In my school I will go to _____ to see

_____.

I will use a special pass to get out of class. I will

_____ to calm myself.

I have discussed this with my _____,

_____ and s/he agrees with my plan.

Signed_____ (Teacher)

Date:_____

38

How to Communicate Your Needs

Telling others what you feel, want or need can be difficult. But if you are not able to express yourself, you cannot expect others to be able to help you. *Therefore, it is important to communicate your needs as clearly as possible.*

First of all – know what you need.
Make sure you understand what you need.
If you're not sure, go over what is unclear with the help of a parent, teacher, counselor or other trusted adult. *You may also want to check out the the ideas in Successful Strategies, page 59.*

My plan for COMMUNICATING MY NEEDS is to _____

I will_____ will not _____ attend my (IEP) meeting(s) (check one).

If I don't go to the meeting(s), I can tell _____ to give my point of view.

What My Teachers Should Know

Check the answers that apply to you and add others, if necessary.

☐ I can't go from one class or subject to another without a rest.

☐ A rest might be reading or just being away from people.

☐ I can sometimes tell when I am going to explode. If I had a safe, quiet space to go to, the explosion might be avoided.

☐ Even though I am _____ (smart/have a good vocabulary, etc.), I sometimes don't get the obvious. I might try to hide it, act like I don't care, or think I am better than other people, but I could use some understanding and help.

☐ Sometimes I can do things in my head but have a hard time figuring out how I did it. That's why I don't always show the work in math class, for example.

☐ Although I can read quickly and know lots of words, I don't always understand what is going on with the characters in a story – I get the plot and the facts, but maybe not the ideas, conflicts or emotions.

☐ I have very specific interests in books and various subjects. I have trouble reading or learning about things that other people choose for me. I might get stuck and need help to move on.

☐ I hate change, especially when I don't know about it ahead of time.

☐ I might NOT be very flexible.

☐ I tend to see things as black or white. I have trouble seeing the middle ground.

☐ I have trouble paying attention; my mind might wander or I might get "over-focused" and not be able to change activities very easily.

☐ I might act like I don't care about having friends, but I HATE BEING TEASED and would like to be liked and have friends.

☐ I am pretty disorganized; I lose things all the time; I can never find what I need; my locker and book bag are stuffed, but I am afraid to try to do things differently or some-one else's way.

☐ I know I'm different from other kids because I _____

_____

_____.

☐ I'm used to it, and sometimes I feel proud of being different.

For example,

_____

_____

_____.

So a part of me doesn't want to change the way I do things 'cause I wouldn't be so unique any more.

☐ Other: _____

_____

Did We Miss Anything?

Here is your chance to tell the people around you (your parents, your teachers, your brothers and sisters, your relatives, the other kids) any other things about you that you want them to keep in mind.

For example, "I might not look at you when we are talking, but I am listening." Or, "I don't like to be hugged even though I am glad to see you."

Here are some things about me I want to be sure you know:

_____

_____

_____

_____

_____

_____

_____

_____

_____

JOURNAL

THE GOOD NEWS

Things that don't come naturally can be learned.

- This includes social skills, organizational skills and a personal "operating system." Your personal "operating system" is the way you do things: how you get yourself up in the morning, how you remember things, how, when and where you do homework, or chores, etc.

Things that come naturally to me:

_____

_____

_____

_____

_____

Things I've learned from others:

_____

_____

_____

_____

_____

If you know what you want and are willing to try the "un-natural,"
you can accomplish many of your goals.

How to Begin

GET HELP.
Find an adult you trust and feel comfortable with. How about your guidance counselor, a favorite teacher, the special education teacher in your school?

GET INFORMATION.
Get help to understand yourself; this workbook is a great start!

KNOW YOUR GOALS AND DEFINE THE STEPS YOU WILL USE TO ACHIEVE THEM.

My goals are to: _____

_____

_____

To achieve these goals I need to: _____

_____

_____

I plan to start by: _____

_____

_____

COMMUNICATE
Tell your parents and teachers what you need.

FOLLOW THE PATH – EVEN WHEN IT'S NOT "WHAT YOU USUALLY DO."

PLACES TO LOOK FOR MORE INFORMATION

On the Web

On-Line Asperger's Syndrome Information and Support – OASIS
http://www.aspergersyndrome.org

Asperger's Disorder Home Page
http:www.ummed.edu./pub/o/ozbayrak/asperger.html

The Centre for the Study of Autism
http://www.autism.org

Autism Society of America
http://www.autism-society.org/asa_home.html

Autism Network International
http://www.students.uiuc.edu/~bordner/ani.html
http://www.aspennj.org/
http://www.orgsites.com/md/asperger_syndrome_info/

Asperger Association of New England
http://www.aane.org

Some Books You Might Like

(Your school or local library may have these books)

Asperger Syndrome and Adolescence: Helping Preteens & Teens Get Ready for the Real World
by Teresa Bolick (Fair Winds Press, 2001)

Asperger's Huh? A Child's Perspective
by Rosina Schnurr et al. (Anisor Publishing, 1999)

Asperger's Syndrome, The Universe and Everything: Kenneth's Book
by Kenneth Hall (Jessica Kingsley Publishers, 2001)

Freaks, Geeks and Asperger Syndrome: A User Guide to Adolescence
by Luke Jackson, Tony Attwood (Foreword) (Jessica Kingsley Publishers, 2002)

Practical Solutions to Everyday Challenges for Children with Asperger Syndrome by Haley
Morgan Myles (Autism Asperger Publishing Company, 2002)

What is Asperger Syndrome, and How Will It Affect Me? A Guide for Young People by
Martine Ives (The National Autistic Society, 2001; distributed in the United States
by the Autism Asperger Publishing Company)

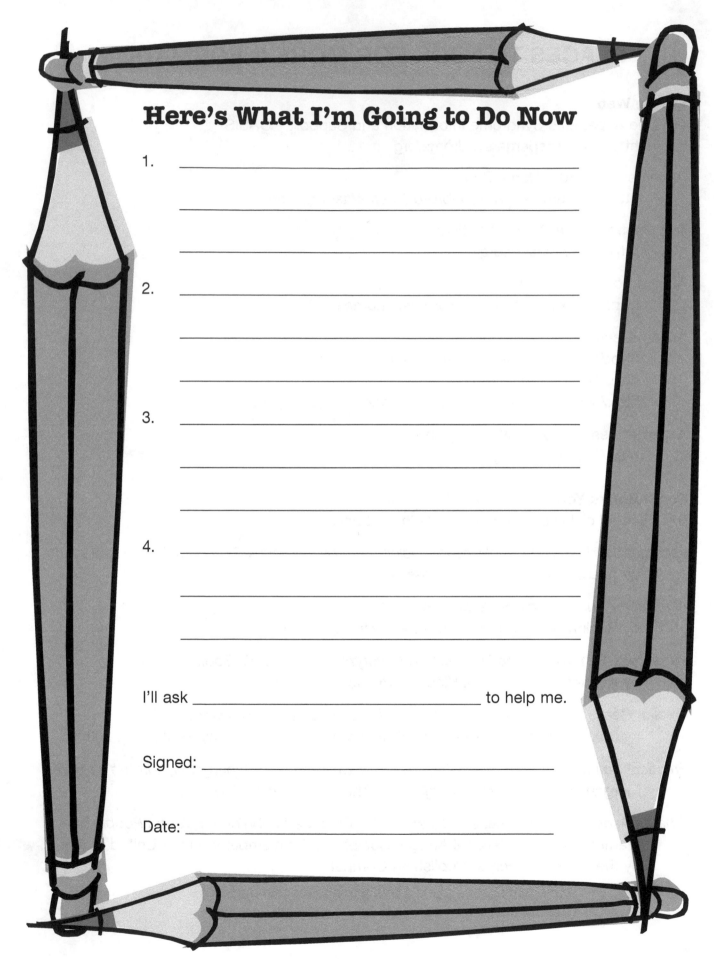

Here's What I'm Going to Do Now

1. _____

_____

_____

2. _____

_____

_____

3. _____

_____

_____

4. _____

_____

_____

I'll ask _____ to help me.

Signed: _____

Date: _____

A PERSONAL PORTRAIT

I hope you have learned a lot about yourself and about Asperger Syndrome. AS is only one aspect of the "whole you." Like everyone else, you are a complex combination of strengths and weaknesses.

Celebrate yourself and what you have learned.

Here's how:

- Create a "portrait" poem of yourself using your name.

  For example my name is **Ellen Korin**, so my poem would look something like this:

  Enjoys helping others, eats chocolate

  Loves to read, to learn, to travel

  Lives in Massachusetts but loves New York

  Entertains new ideas and tries new things

  Not a risk taker, not good at math

  Keeps close to friends and family

  Open-minded, open-hearted

  Remembers

  Is really kind of shy

  Needs lots of alone time.

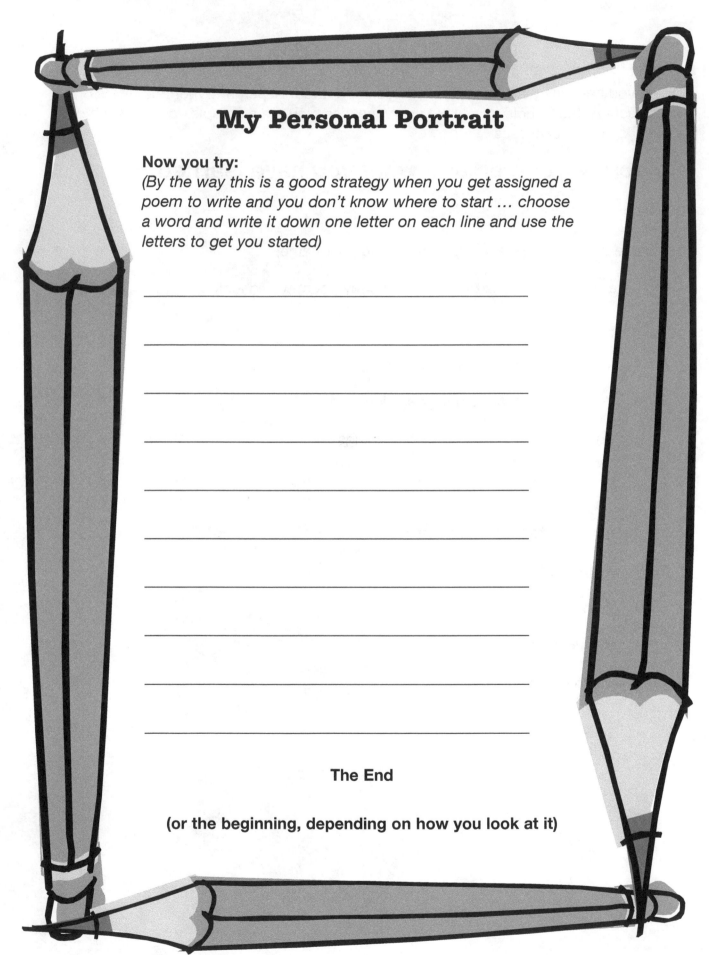

My Personal Portrait

Now you try:
(By the way this is a good strategy when you get assigned a poem to write and you don't know where to start ... choose a word and write it down one letter on each line and use the letters to get you started)

_____

_____

_____

_____

_____

_____

_____

_____

The End

(or the beginning, depending on how you look at it)

PART 3
SUCCESSFUL
STRATEGIES

SOME GOOD IDEAS THAT REALLY WORK AT SCHOOL!

- Make sure you write down your assignments in your assignment book.

- If writing is hard for you, or if your handwriting is hard to read:
  - Get help from the teacher or aide
  - Use a mini-cassette recorder to record your words
  - Have a homework buddy in each class who can give you the information later
  - Visit the teacher's website
  - Ask the teacher to give you assignments in writing

- For long-term assignments, write the assignment on ALL the days between the day assigned and the due date but change colors to increasingly bright colors to signify that you are getting closer to the due date.

- CHECK YOUR ASSIGNMENT BOOK BEFORE YOU LEAVE SCHOOL (so you can remember what books to take home) and CHECK IT AGAIN WHEN YOU GET HOME.

- BEFORE YOU LEAVE HOME IN THE MORNING, CHECK TO MAKE SURE YOU HAVE ALL THE THINGS YOU NEED FOR THE DAY.

  The following checklist can help.

BEFORE YOU LEAVE HOME IN THE MORNING	YES	DATE
☐ HOMEWORK		
☐ TEXTBOOKS		
☐ BINDER		
☐ NOTICES/PERMISSION SLIPS		
☐ LUNCH OR LUNCH MONEY		
☐ READING BOOK		
☐ GYM CLOTHES/SNEAKERS		
☐ OTHER		
☐ (DID I MENTION HOMEWORK)		
☐ OTHER		
BEFORE YOU LEAVE SCHOOL	YES	DATE
☐ BINDER		
☐ ASSIGNMENTS – WRITTEN AND UNDERSTOOD		
☐ NEEDED HANDOUTS		
☐ NEEDED TEXTBOOKS		
☐ NOTICES/PERMISSION SLIPS		
☐ LUNCHBOX		
☐ CLOTHING ITEMS, INCLUDING GYMWEAR TO WASH		
☐ ASSIGNMENTS – WRITTEN AND UNDERSTOOD		
☐ INSTRUMENTS		
☐ PLAN FOR OBTAINING INFORMATION IF NEEDED		
☐ OTHER		
☐ OTHER		
☐ OTHER		

- Have a folder or a section in a folder for each subject, and perhaps a homework folder. Have a separate folder for notices, newsletters, notes from the teacher or principal, etc. Make a practice of giving notices (checking the notices folder) to your parents just before you start your homework.

- Try using an accordion file instead of a binder (make sure it's one that opens wide enough to put papers in easily and that it has enough sections).

- If you are having trouble concentrating in class, take a short break – get a drink, go to the bathroom, ask to be the errand person who takes notes to the office, and so on.

- Use Wet Wipes™ to refresh yourself.

- If you don't like to be called on unexpectedly in class, ask the teacher to give you notice: "I'm going to be back to you in a minute to ask you about_____."

51

SOME GOOD IDEAS THAT REALLY WORK AT HOME!

- If you are a daydreamer or a procrastinator, or if you tend to become distracted, especially by the computer, don't work in isolation (in your room). Work where someone will notice if you drift off and will bring it to your attention

- Make a schedule of when you will do homework each day, taking into consideration appointments, activities, chores, etc.

- Try your schedule out for a week and revise if needed.

- Then stick to it!!

- Set up your work area with a place for everything:
  - Pens, pencils, erasers and white-out
  - Paper, graph paper, colored paper
  - Markers and colored pencils
  - Scissors and glue
  - Folders
  - File box or cabinet

  IMPORTANT RULE: WHATEVER YOU TAKE OUT TO USE, REPLACE TO THE EXACT LOCATION AS SOON AS YOU ARE FINISHED USING IT.

- Clean out your binder and backpack at a set time each week. Sometimes it helps to have someone help.

- File papers you want to keep but don't need right away in your file box (or similar place) at home.

- Have a homework bin for keeping graded homework.

- Throw out any unneeded papers or other trash.

- Replenish the supplies at your workspace at the same time on a regular basis.

- When you do your homework, follow these steps:
  1. Start with the most difficult subject.
  2. Set a timer for about 20 minutes.
  3. CONCENTRATE.
  4. When you're done, take a 5-minute break.
  5. Go on to the next most challenging assignment, and so on. See also page 54.

- Make a weekly calendar that includes all your appointments and commitments. Identify a good time each day for homework.

Example of Weekly Homework Calendar

TIME	MONDAY	TUESDAY	WEDNESDAY	THURSDAY	FRIDAY
3:00 PM	CLUB	HOMEWORK			HOMEWORK
4:00 PM		HOMEWORK		SPORT	HOMEWORK
5:00 PM	HOMEWORK	HOMEWORK	RELIGION		HOMEWORK
6:00 PM	DINNER	DINNER	DINNER	DINNER	DINNER
7:00 PM	FINISH HOMEWORK		HOMEWORK	HOMEWORK	
8:00 PM			HOMEWORK	HOMEWORK	
9:00 PM					

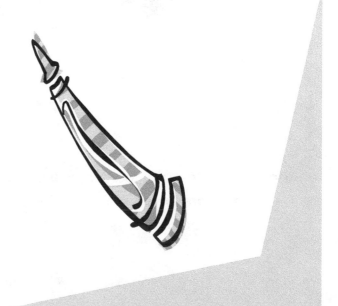

Homework "Wonder Wheel"

Start with the hardest subject or the subject you like the least. Go on to the next hardest subject for you, and so on, so that when you get tired you are working on your easiest or most enjoyable subject.

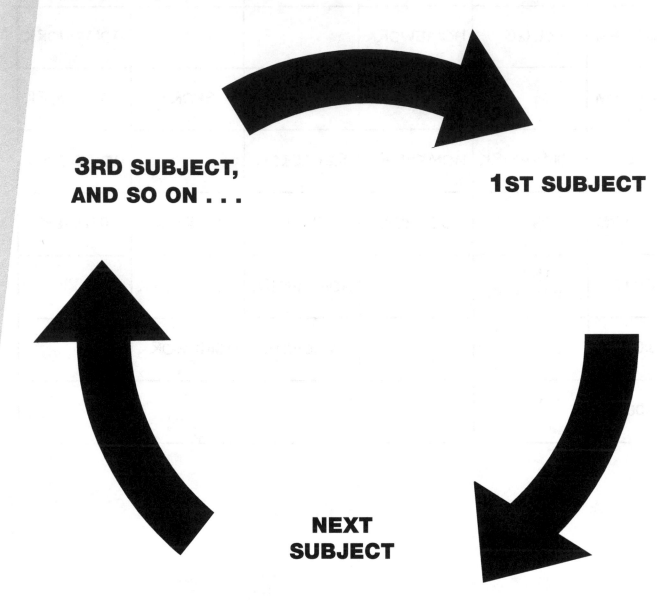

3RD SUBJECT, AND SO ON . . .

1ST SUBJECT

NEXT SUBJECT

Alternative Method: You can also do your homework assignments in the order in which the subjects are in your schedule for the next school day. It is NOT a good idea to rely on being able to complete assignments in a free block or study hall before a class.

YOUR "EMERGENCY KIT"

Let's say you are ...
- on a long road trip
- at a family get-together
- traveling by airplane or boat
- doing tons of errands with your family
- going shopping

These are times when you might feel "trapped" or stressed by all that's going on around you. For example, you may need to interact with others, make sudden decisions or be delayed while waiting for others, etc.

This is when you need an EMERGENCY KIT – a set of personal "soothers" and stress reducers.

How to Make an Emergency Kit

Pick the things that are most soothing for you:
- ✔ a book you love
- ✔ a CD or DVD
- ✔ a handheld game player
- ✔ a stuffed animal
- ✔ a favorite pillow
- ✔ some special treats
- ✔ earplugs or an eye mask
- ✔ iPod or MP3 player

Pack these items in your backpack and use them to help "escape" the stress.

MELTDOWN MONITOR

Use the MELTDOWN MONITOR to help you avoid a meltdown, or at least make it less severe. In the first column list what you are feeling: a little annoyed or frustrated, anxious to get your point across, etc. Then indicate the level or degree of upset and what you can do to prevent getting more upset. If you think in terms of 3 levels:

1. Getting Upset
2. Upset
3. Meltdown,

you should be able to notice and list the feelings (emotional and physical) that let you know you are on the way to a meltdown.

SAMPLE MELTDOWN MONITOR

FEELING	LEVEL	WHAT TO DO
Feeling like you have butterflies in your stomach	1	Go for a drink and get some air
Frustrated	1– 2	Take some downtime – use a soother
Upset	2	Low lights, quiet space, calming music
Having a meltdown	3	If at school, parents called – may need to go home. If not, trusted adult stand by to assist in recovery

The Meltdown Monitor above is an example only. Please design your own as part of your meltdown prevention/reduction plan.

Develop a Plan

- First you and your family members will need to agree upon a quiet, safe spot (your room?) where you can go to calm yourself.

- Once you get there, you can use some of your best soothers and distractors (video game, music, TV) to calm yourself. You might need to get rid of some of your anger by talking (or yelling) out loud or into a tape recorder. Maybe it would help to write all your thoughts in a letter or to use a diary or journal, or to call an ally, mentor, therapist or coach.

After everyone agrees to this plan, TRY IT! REVISE IT! USE IT!

There are things you can do to prevent a meltdown.

- Take breaks to avoid a build-up of stress; spend some quiet time several times a day (in the counselor's office, the special education teacher's room, the nurse) in a private location. Relax, "catch your breath," *decompress*.

DON'T WAIT UNTIL YOU THINK YOU NEED A BREAK. TAKE THE BREAKS TO PREVENT THE BUILD-UP OF STRESS THAT LEADS TO OVERLOAD AND MELTDOWN.

- Learn to notice when a meltdown is coming. After a meltdown write down all the thoughts and feelings you remember so that you can begin to recognize the signs the next time you start to get agitated (see page 56).

- Arrange for a pass you can use to get out of class if you begin to feel overwhelmed or upset. You want to avoid yelling or crying in class. You can use the pass to go to a quiet, safe, private place where an understanding adult can help.

- When you feel that you will "lose it," GO to your "safe space" and helping adult ... and talk or yell or read or play the computer or turn down the lights and listen to soothing music or meditate or do a relaxation routine – whatever works best for you.

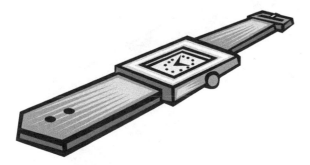

GREAT IDEAS THAT REALLY WORK!!

To stay cool at school:
- Go at your own pace – don't rush.
- Take pre-arranged breaks.
- Use the helping adults to support you when problems arise.
- Go to a safe space to think things through.
- Practice self-calming techniques such as meditation or relaxation.
- Learn how to tell when you're about to explode.
- HAVE A PLAN.
- USE YOUR PLAN.

Once you know more about what you need,
let people know how they can help.

You will need ways to let people know what you need and how they can be of help to you. One important way is to participate in the meetings at school. You can have a say in what help you get, what accommodations you need, what gets written in your IEP (do you know what that is? It's your Individualized Educational Program, and it tells what services – extra help – you are entitled to, what helps you learn, etc.). The IEP is a very important document and you have very important information to contribute to it. Bring your workbook to meetings so you can refer to what you have learned or show people what you have written. Also, people at the meeting may have some observations or information that you can include in your workbook.

Another way to communicate your needs is to talk to your parents or other trusted adult and ask them to help you let teachers and others know what is on your mind.

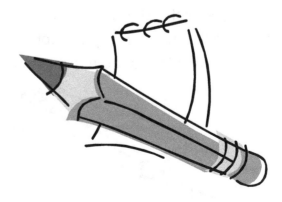

IF YOU WANT TO COMMUNICATE DIRECTLY

- Write a script to help you explain. Use a summary sheet to help you.

  For example:

  I have concerns about: _____

  _____

  _____

  I wondered if it would be possible to: _____

  _____

  _____

  It would help me if: _____

  _____

  _____

  I would appreciate it if: _____

  _____

  _____

  Something I thought you should know: _____

  _____

  _____

- If you don't think you can speak directly to the person, can you:
  - write a note?
  - leave a voicemail?
  - write an email?
  - record on a tape?

  If these options don't work, find a mentor who can help you or actually transmit the information for you.

- Use a communication journal with parents, teachers, and siblings.

OTHER IDEAS AND THOUGHTS

AAPC Publishing
6448 Vista Dr.
Shawnee, KS 66218
www.aapcpublishing.net

CPSIA information can be obtained
at www.ICGtesting.com
Printed in the USA
LVHW051404180522
719075LV00009B/663